DESTINED TO BE HERE

For He will see you through

BOBBIE WILLIS

ISBN Number: 978-0-578-719702

Power of Purpose Publishing
3355 Lenox Rd
Atlanta, Ga 30326
Www.PopPublishing.com

DESTINED
TO BE HERE

DEDICATION

First and foremost, I thank God for His grace and this amazing opportunity to share my story.

I dedicate this book in memory of my deceased dad, Moses Kincaide, sister Teresa Kincaide-Moore, and brother Larry Kincaide.

To my soulmate and husband of 21 years, Ronnie Layne Willis, Sr.: Thank you for being so patient, dependable and inspiring in our marriage and with our two beautiful children. RJ and Gabbie, you two are my heartbeat.

I want to thank my entire family for being so supportive and motivational, especially my 94-year-old granny Willie Ann Kincaide, my mom Caldonia Kincaide, my sister Lisa Rhymes, and brother Tyrone Logan.

Lastly, I dedicate this book to my god mom, Rev. Sarah Martin. Even though she has made her transition to be with the Lord, she still lives through the influence, love and wisdom she imparted to me and all those she took under her wing.

Thanks

Crystal Williams & Mrs. Claudette Avery- Pre-Sale Book
Launch Event Coordinators

Syreeta Kee – Personal Consultant

Petey Swearengen- Photographer

Sha Durr- Makeup Artist

Claudette Avery- Hair Stylist for Photo Shoot

TABLE OF CONTENTS

Shy But Gifted   11

From Stressed To Blessed   17

Heartbroken, But I Made It   25

Do What You Have To Do   33

God's Favor   41

I Had A Reason To Press   49

Reflections And Memories   61

Why Am I Here   69

SHY BUT GIFTED

I remember it clearly; it was a hot summer day in 1980. I was a 6-year-old girl that was scared to talk to anyone in my classroom, in my church, and in large settings. I had a lot that I wanted to say in my head, but I didn't have enough confidence to say it from my mouth. My teachers saw untapped potential and a bright future within me. As a result, many of them put me in the front of the class. I would never ask to take the lead on anything. However, my teachers said that I was a natural leader. I was quiet, but they noticed my interaction with my classmates, especially when we were divided into groups. At first, I would be quiet and a little scared, but once I became comfortable, I talked and listened to the other students in my group very well. Soon it became the norm, rather than the exception, that I would be nominated to be the leader for the group. The leader was automatically the spokesperson for the group and here is the shy girl being thrust into this position. One day, I asked one of my teachers why was I always asked to lead my group. My teacher replied, "You are gifted." When I went back to my seat, I really started thinking about what my teacher said, and I began searching for my gifts. I pondered. Later, I realized that if I was gifted that meant I have exceptional talent and natural ability. I thought to myself. That is exactly me! Even though I was never one who thought I had to imitate anyone else, I gained a sense of pride in being exceptional. Not only was I encouraged, but my grandmother and grandfather were inspired as well. I would hear them praying in the midnight hour for me to have great success and to be able to do things that they never got a chance to do.

My friend's mom would walk to our house every Sunday morning so she, my sister and I could walk to church together. I volunteered to join the choir, but I was too afraid to sing a song. This played out for quite a while, until I was introduced to the pastor, Presiding Elder Sarah Martin. She adopted me as her spiritual daughter, and I adopted her as my spiritual mother. We quickly developed a spiritual connection. She took me under her wings and began to minister to me daily. My confidence increased enormously because she helped me understand that I was different and had something special to offer. With the increased confidence, my natural ability rose to another level. I had often been told that I was a natural leader, but now I started to see and believe it. I began to quote Proverbs 18:16 which says, "A man's gift maketh room for him, and bringeth him before great men." One day God revealed a gift to me that I never imagined, one that was even more than a gift. It was a high calling. God had called me to preach His gospel. How would this work? I knew that you couldn't preach if you didn't open your mouth. I didn't know if I could do it, but God gave me the power that I needed.

I preached my first sermon and months later I went to college at Alcorn State University for four years. I traveled back and forth home so I could attend church, but I couldn't commit to anything because I had to go back to campus. I kept a close relationship with my pastor the four years that I was in college. When I graduated from college, my spiritual mother and pastor chartered a bus so my church family and friends could attend my graduation. My father in the gospel, Rev. Sammy Townes, drove the bus. This meant the world to me. I was finally feeling the love and sense of belonging that I had desperately needed and wanted for so long. These people embraced me and our common love for God and agape love for each other made us family. Not only was I excited to receive my degree, they were genuinely proud and overjoyed as well. That was another gift from the Lord.

Although I struggled financially while I was in college, I made it. Things were hard and I could have given up, but knowing I had purpose caused me to hold on and keep the faith. I knew I had to prepare myself to live a better life than I was accustomed to living, even if it meant scraping by then. Fortunately, I had a spiritual mother who prayed me through each and every challenge. I do know one thing.

I lost my taste for noodles because I ate them so much in college.

After graduation, I had to get back to what I loved, and that was preaching and teaching the word of God. I learned why God had me to quote Proverbs 18:16. It was because He had already planned my journey, paved the way and opened hearts and doors that provoked men and women of high ranks in the gospel to invite me to preach and teach in their churches. His favor began to overtake me. Only God could take a young, shy girl who was mortified when asked to sing and make her a leader in spreading the Gospel of Jesus Christ. I still get nervous before I preach or speak at different engagements, but after I pray and meditate on God's word and His goodness, I get the peace that I need to go forth.

My spiritual mom and I traveled together after I returned home. We went to places like Louisiana, Georgia, Chicago, Chattanooga, Detroit, Texas, Arkansas, North Carolina, St. Louis, Virginia Beach, and Washington, D.C., etc. I didn't notice it at the time, but she was giving me exposure and providing life lessons all along the way. I owe her so much. She didn't just help me to have confidence in myself, she helped to build my confidence in the Lord. Through her, I found out that once you get a spiritual relationship with the Lord, you know that He can bring you out of anything. I've had the opportunity to pastor two churches in the West TN & Mississippi Conference. The first church I pastored was Brassell Chapel A.M.E. Zion church. The church that I'm currently pastoring is Eureka A.M.E. Zion church. I've been pastoring there almost eight years. Never in my wildest dreams did I think that a timid girl like me would be leading anybody. Jeremiah 29:11 "For I know the plans I have for you, 'declares the LORD', plans to prosper you and not harm you, plans to give you hope and a future." God knows our future. Just because you have accepted limitations on your life doesn't mean God has. If God has anointed your gift for His glory, no conditions can destroy it. By the same token, you must surrender, be teachable and be willing to use it. We all have natural abilities and exceptional talents in some area or another, and we can use them to help us to be exceptional leaders.

FROM STRESSED TO BLESSED

I will never forget August 8, 1988. That was the day my father passed away. My mom was left with four children to raise. I prayed that my dad's funeral would be over as soon as possible so the healing process could begin.

Well, the healing never came for my mom. She began to drink heavily every day. She would constantly yell out to us, "Why did your daddy leave me?" Things became so bad that we wouldn't see our mom for two to three weeks at a time. My sister and I had to grow up instantaneously. Responsibility found us! We found ourselves managing a household and practically had to raise our younger sister and brother. While we wanted to do things like the other teenagers, we simply could not. If we did, who would be there for them?

There was pressure to try to make sure that we had food in the house so we could eat. My older sister and I made sure that our brother and sister were safe both at school and at home. We would get to school some days and the other students would be discussing what they heard about our mother. On top of being stressed, we would be extremely embarrassed.

Because of daddy's death, my mom had an immeasurable amount of anger and rage built up and pent up inside of her. She started acting out and her behavior became so unpredictable. One night, she threw a fit and broke every table, lamp, picture, and dish that was in the house. We were afraid to invite any of our friends to our home because we didn't know what she was going to do next. I think the police department grew tired of us calling. Yes, she had to go to jail several times. It hurt me to the core of my being to see her get in that police car, but she had gotten out of control.

I would sit around and wonder what it would be like to have love in our home. I envisioned so many scenarios, but something always happened to snap me right back into the reality that seemed to be our lot in life. Those thoughts and visions encouraged me some days, but some nights I would go to bed crying and continue to cry all night long. It seemed like other kids around us had it all while we had nothing.

I knew there was a better way. I just had to figure out how to get to it. My sister and I prayed that God would save our mother. However, at that time, the more we prayed the worse our mom's behavior became.

Trying to hide what was going on in our home was stressful to say the least. Although a lot of people already knew, trying to cover and keep things at bay started to take a toll. My mother would go to the clubs, even on weeknights, and wouldn't come home until the club's lights were on and the doors were closed. One night really stands out in my head; I will never forget it. Hearing her come in after her night out, I woke up. I got up and saw a blaze down our hallway. My mom had set our house on fire! I started screaming telling everybody to get out of the house. Fortunately, my uncle decided to stay the night. He heard me scream and came running out of the bedroom. Once he saw what was going on, he tried to suffocate the flames. From the door, I saw a guy walking down the street. I stopped him and asked him to come and help my uncle extinguish the fire. He ran in to help. Between the two of them, the fire was put out and we were safe. I couldn't sleep for days after that happened. Every time I tried to go to sleep, I would think about that blaze of fire that I saw in our hallway.

All things considered, we kept praying and trying to help my mom. My sister and I asked our mom to go to church with us several times. She never would go. Surprisingly, one night she came to revival. She had even more of a surprise, she was drunk! Being so happy that she came at all, I had no idea that she was intoxicated, but she was. Her antics were highly unusual, not to mention inappropriate for church. I was so embarrassed that I almost walked out of the church. After experiencing what I experienced with my mom at revival that night, I made up my mind to never drink anything that would alter my state of mind and make me act like that.

If you think that was enough to spark a change, you are wrong. Oh, it was far from over. The incidents continued. One night in particular, my sisters, brother and I were sitting in the living room when we heard the kitchen door close. It was our mom. She was in a rage about something. She started throwing everything she could get her hands on across the room. My sisters and I had a code that we would say if we needed to react quickly. When we said the code, we knew not to ask questions because it was time to respond. My baby sister said the code that meant to duck. We knew flying objects were near anytime anyone used it. When she used it, I reacted just in time to avoid being hit with a broom! My mom tried to hit me with a broom. She missed me, but she knocked all the pictures off the wall. I kept replaying that moment back and forth in my head. I could not take it anymore. I told my mom that in order to keep the respect that I had for her, I had to leave. She said, "Bye." I prayed so hard that night. It was then that I released my mom unto the Lord.

I moved in with my grandmother. The whole time I was there, I constantly worried about my sisters and brother. I kept in touch with them daily, but I didn't go to the house. I didn't hate my mom, but I could not tolerate being under the same roof with her any longer. No children should have to put up with the torture that we had encountered. Even though I was deeply hurt, I kept praying. I just believed that one day she would change, and she did.

We prayed and prayed for a change. It didn't happen until after I finished college, but I still was happy. It was a miracle no doubt. One day she made up in her mind that she wasn't going to smoke or drink again, and she didn't. She started going to church and to this day, she attends our home church every Sunday. Sometimes I will pick her up to go to church with me. We stay out all day and she seems to enjoy every minute of it. She doesn't even get in a hurry to go back home. She's gotten her glow back that she once had. I praise God every day for her change.

I want everyone to know that if you don't give up on God, He won't give up on you. If by chance you are stressing about something, God can turn it around as your blessing.

HEARTBROKEN, BUT I MADE IT

I've had a lot of heartbreak in my life. Health conditions, broken relationships, less than ideal family issues and the loss of my father, my brother, and my sister topped the list. I didn't think it could get any worse. However, one morning my husband had gone into town and returned. He was yelling at the top of his lungs, "Bobbie, where are you?" I said reluctantly, "I'm in the bathroom." Slightly relieved, he asked me to come out and told me everybody had been trying to reach me. Startled, my eyes bucked wide as saucers. A million things raced through my head while he seemed to be mustering up the courage to tell me what happened. He finally said, "Rev. Martin died early this morning." I asked him, "What Rev.

Martin?" I was hoping he would say someone that I didn't know, but sadly he said, "Rev. Sarah Martin." The Rev. Martin that was my pastor, godmother, friend, counselor, confidante, teacher, spiritual advisor, and so much more. When my husband told me, I dropped to the floor. I was crying uncontrollably. I said, "My phone didn't ring." I just knew my nose was going to start bleeding. It bleeds every time I get really upset and that is describing how I felt at that moment very mildly. Sure enough, it started bleeding. Trying to help, my husband told me to hold my head back. I knew that was a mistake, but I was too upset to tell him. I just did what he asked. When I did that, blood started to come from my mouth with a gurgling sound. My husband almost lost it. He automatically assumed there was something seriously wrong and rushed me to the hospital. Although everything checked out fine physically, I was not. When I finally had a chance to look at my cell phone, I had ten missed calls. At that moment, I thanked God for His protection. He did not want me to receive any of those calls about my godmother's death while my husband wasn't there with me.

Everyone knew that I was close to her, so everyone had tried to contact me. I just could not engage with anyone. I was in disbelief. I had just talked to her the day before. I had to get some sort of grasp on things, so I asked my husband to take me to her house. Since I was so emotionally drained and physically weak, he suggested that we wait until the next morning. I agreed, but I didn't get any sleep that night. I felt helpless. She taught me everything I knew about the Lord, how to be a real Christian and how to be a good leader. It was her teaching and prayers that got me through the dark days and nights that I had already gone through. I watched how she carried herself as a woman and as an ambassador for the Lord. She told me to always protect my character. She taught me what the bible really means. I received the power of the Holy Spirit under her leadership. I stayed at her house many days and nights. A hair stylist by trade, she styled my hair one time and that was enough for me. It became a running joke, and we laughed about that hair style all the time. A lot of people thought that she let me get away with everything at the church, but she didn't. She was harder on me than anybody in the whole church. She told me that I expect more from you because you are always with me, learning how to allow the Lord to order your steps in His word. She always reminded me that the only bible that some may ever see is the one they see living in us in our daily walk with the Lord.

Rev. Martin and I traveled the highways late in the midnight hour going back and forth to different preaching engagements. She had her share of health issues just as I had. She even had a heart attack once, but she survived. That heart attack boosted her praise all the more. She walked by faith. I witnessed it for myself. She used to plan to go to different institutes, conferences all over the world and would not have any money. I asked her how much money she had once when she was planning to go to one of our General Conferences in the A.M.E. Zion church. She said, "Nothing." I said to myself how is she going to get a flight to North Carolina without any money. Her phone started ringing off the hook. People were asking her to stop by and pick up checks or cash so she could buy food or whatever she needed. Her faith provoked her provision. She went to North Carolina, participated in the General

Conference and came back safely. Her faith and trust helped build my faith. Seeing her do it made me believe that I could do it, too. On one occasion, she and my god sister, Tammy, were getting ready to go on a trip and Tammy told my godmother that the Lord told her that I could go on the trip, too. I was looking at my god sister and saying God didn't tell me anything like that. I didn't question it, but all I know is that I went with them. I was given four hundred dollars for spending money by our current Bishop. I came back home with money that I didn't have when I left to go. One thing for sure is that she had my back. We didn't always see eye to eye, but that is life. At the end of the day, all I had to do was call her. I used to get mistreated because of our close relationship, but that same relationship nurtured me, and gave me the heart to do what was right.

Rev. Martin officiated our wedding. Knowing we had a tight bond, my husband would call her when he thought I did not do what I should do . He knew she would talk to me. I guess that was good. In fact, I know it was good. She always told me that she wouldn't be around all the time.

That went in one ear and out the other because I didn't believe she would ever die. I wasn't thinking that because I had witnessed her at death's door so many times, and she had always beaten death.

Two weeks before she died, she called me and told me that she needed to meet me so we could sit down and talk. We lived about forty miles from each other. While I did talk to her during those two weeks, it was just casual conversation. To this day, I wonder what she wanted to discuss with me.

I went to her homegoing celebration and I cried the whole time. I actually don't remember how I got home. My eyes were swollen tight from crying so much. I almost became physically ill at the funeral. I was doing well until I looked into her face. I could not get the expression of her still face out of my head. I had so many people call me to make sure that I made it home after that funeral. Most did not see me because I did not linger. I went straight home. Yes, I was depressed for a while. I thought that I didn't have anyone else that I could depend on like her. After all, she taught me everything that I knew. Most of her friends were my friends. The loss of my godmother and pastor of over twenty years took me down a lonely path for a while. Fortunately, one night the Lord spoke to me. I started to remember what Rev. Martin taught me, and that was how to pray. I began to pray and call on the Lord. He brought me out of that valley of dry bones and restored my hope and strength. From personal experience, I confidently encourage anyone that has lost someone or something close to them to know that with God's help, you can make it.

DO WHAT YOU HAVE TO DO

People see my glory, but they don't know the details of my story. That is one of the reasons that I decided to write this book. I have had many long nights and grueling days for a variety of reasons. Some nights I am up all night long because of the ruptured disk in my lower back. It is so painful that I can barely turn over in bed. It may slow me down, but I do not let the pain stop me from preaching and teaching God's word. I want to be able to encourage others to keep pushing even when they are hurting or not feeling well. Pushing forward may require extra, but it is worth it. It takes me time to get up, get a bath and then get dressed. My kids know that I do not like to rush. They always ask me, "Mamma, why does it take you so long to get dressed?" I always tell them that it takes time to look differently from how you feel. Just because you do not feel good, doesn't mean that you have to look like it. I have been through a lot. If I did not know the Lord, I would not have made it this far, and I probably would look like what I have been through. It was certainly God's grace that has brought me and kept me.

Regardless of the obstacles, you have to do what you have to do to get where you need to be. You have people that will judge you because you look too blessed n their eyes. They are not aware that there were many days that I did not have a penny in my pocket. Nobody knew and it was not obvious when you looked at me. That is a result of my faith walk. I believe that when I pray that all things are possible through Jesus, who is my keeper. I almost didn't graduate from college because I had a low F grade that I could not pull up by numerical calculations. I paid someone, with the little money that I had, to tutor me. The class professor was on a different level and not in a good way. He did not appear to believe in anything except himself. I was afraid to even talk to him. The second semester was about to end, and I had to submit my documentation. I was sure that I was going to fail. One day after class, I slipped a letter under my advisor's door, telling him my predicament and that I did not know what to do because I was intimidated by my instructor. Two days had gone by and I still did not hear from my advisor. I had to go to the building where my advisor's office was the next day. As soon as I entered the building, he saw me and asked me to come into his office. I went to his office as he requested. He said, "I read your letter and I have been crying for two days, trying to figure out something." He was trying to help, but God had already intervened. I ended up with a D in the class. My advisor and I both were jumping up and down. I took that low grade with the highest regards because I knew something high was going to come out of it. Some may ask the question, what is going to come out of you getting this low grade? Well, that low D allowed me to not only graduate on time, but to do it with honors.

I remember the very moment that the doctor told me that I had cancer. I did not have any doubt that I would beat it. Honestly, I just did not want to go through the process. I had watched so many of my family members go through the agonizing pain of this disease. Plus, I had prayed against it for years. Why me? Well, why not me? This, like other ordeals, was preparing me for greater things to come. When I prayed and thought about my two children and my husband, I made up in my mind that I would fight to the best of my ability in God's strength, so I could be here with them. It is a fact that we will all be faced with trials and tribulations in life that are not easy to deal with, but when it's over we will be rewarded. I consider still being here thirteen years later one of the greatest rewards. It has not been easy, but I had a choice to fight or fold. Some choices were harder than others, but the choice to fight for life was a no-brainer.

As I have previously related, Hawaii had been my dream vacation destination. On the other hand, I did not want to fly over the Pacific Ocean on a flight almost nine hours from my location. Sometimes sacrifice, change and regrouping are necessary. When I received the opportunity to do a work detail there, I had to put my fears aside and change my mindset because I could not chicken out of this chance. I had to really pray, but I regrouped and was on my way. It may be unbelievable, but I did not leave my seat any time during the entire flight. My seat was next to some young kid that had become intoxicated from drinking gin and juice. I blocked him out of my mind by concentrating on the clouds and the water. Every time I looked out the widow, I could see beautiful blue water. After what seemed like an eternity, we landed in Hawaii. When I stood up on the plane, I fell to the floor because my legs had gotten weak from sitting so many hours. Why did I share this? The moral of the story is that I had a desire that was met with an opportunity. The desire was personal, but the opportunity was afforded by my job. This was a setup from God. He arranged it, but gave me the choice to accept or decline it. I did not want to take that long flight, but I had to if I did not want to miss the dream of a lifetime.

Decisions sometimes create mistakes. We all make them, but we have to be sure we learn from them. There is nothing wrong with falling. But when we fall, it is an absolute must that we get back up again. Many of us do not reach our full potential because we are so worried about what people will say or think. For years, I lived my life trying to be careful so people would not talk about me or make accusations about me. Can you guess what I found out? Being careful did not help. I was talked about for doing good and for doing bad. I asked God to help me in that area because I was losing focus trying to conform to the appearance of good all the time. I eventually made up my mind that I was going to live my life to the fullest for the Lord despite what others thought or disliked about me and who preferred not to support me. I admonish everyone to do what you must do for the Kingdom of God. If you make a mistake, there will always be one memory that lingers, but it should not stop your progress.

When my husband and I became engaged, we immediately set a wedding date. The closer it got to the wedding, the more stressed I grew. I asked God why my spirit was so uneasy about the wedding date we chose. One morning He spoke to me. He spoke to me just as clear as day. He said, "I want you all to get married, but not on that date." I knew my husband-to-be did not want to hear that. I prayed about it, and then I told him. He said that he was hurt and disappointed, but he wanted to make sure that I had peace. We told our families and friends. I was grilled really hard by my family. One family member asked me why I changed the date; They said that I was not right. I told them I had prayed, and the Lord told me to change the date. When I said that, they then asked me if I was sure that it was the Lord who told me that. Yes, there was some opposition and speculation, but my husband and I did have a wonderful ceremony on June 5, 1999, complete with family and friends. It was hard for me to change our initial wedding date, but I was not going against what the Lord had said to me. It may be hard to make certain changes, but you do what is best for you. You are the one who must deal with the resulting consequences. Do not let others push you into something that you do not have peace about, and if you hear from God, that automatically settles things. God has been too good for me to turn my back on him and I cannot disregard His leading. It is my responsibility to let men and women of all nations see my dedication and obedience in serving Him until the day I die.

GOD'S FAVOR

God favored me. That is undoubtedly why I am here today. I have been through storms and rain, but I made it. I beat cancer, overcame other health challenges, and I am still on this battlefield for the Lord. It was my trials that made me strong. There were many that started out with me, but some have gone astray or on to be with the Lord. Many times, I thought I was leaving this earth as well, but every time the devil tried to knock me down with sickness, pain, hurt, or rejection, the Lord always came and continues to come to my rescue.

Although I have witnessed the Lord making ways where there were no ways in sight for me, sometimes I still feel like people think that I never have fear or feel like giving up, but I do. However, when I think of how good God has been to me, I cannot quit. His favor may be unmerited, but it comes with responsibility. When you have God's favor on your life, some will reject you and act differently towards you than other people. When people see that you are blessed, they do not want to help you. God's favor also comes with a cost. I have walked in meetings and seen people talking and laughing, but when I get close to them, they will move away or stop talking altogether. I remember one time I was in the checkout line to pay for several books. The cashier reached over me to check out the next person behind me. I asked her, as politely as I could, if she saw me standing in line with all those items in my hand. She did not have a suitable explanation. It does not cost a thing to be nice or fair, but having favor sometimes causes you to choose appropriate responses over reaction to wrong treatment. I am thankful that I realized it is not me, it is the spirit of God that is intimidating to people. When people are not on the same level as you, they have a tendency to misunderstand you.

Many will mistreat you and then walk around as if the world owes them something.

God has been too good to me for me to turn around now for any reason. I recently read a passage that explained favor so well. It said that favor means chosen with gifts. I know I am chosen, and I do have gifts. I have His Holy Spirit. I have the gift of tongues, and I have healing hands. Nevertheless, I only use them when the Lord says to use them, not for show or entertainment.

There are many instances that have prompted me to use my God-given gifts. Early in my walk with Christ, my mom became ill and could not walk. At 2:00 a.m. in the morning, she scrambled around and crawled to my bed, called my name and told me she could not walk. Without even thinking, I took my right hand and immediately put it on her legs, calling on the Lord to heal her situation. Before long, she walked out of my room. I got back in bed and started to think about what had just happened. I knew God had done something amazing, but He had used me. On another occasion at my home church, Mt. Zion A.M.E.

Zion Church in Coffeeville, Mississippi, one of the sisters from the congregation had to be helped up the steps at the church. She used a cane to assist her as well. Her feet had turned, almost meeting each other. I could not believe it because they were not like that the week before. We ended bible study and began prayer service. I laid both my hands on the young lady and she started giving God praise. She walked out that door holding the cane up in the air. Another time, I preached for one of my friends at a Baptist church. When I finished preaching, I noticed that everyone was gathered around an older lady. The lady got up and testified that she had not walked in five years. When she said that, everybody started praising God. My feet became light, and I really began to feel alright. My oldest sister, Lisa, asked me if the lady really said she had not walked in five years. I confirmed that she did, and I was extremely glad that she was there to witness the miracles and wonders of God. The only thing I did was preach the word of God. However, the anointing was in that place. What some people do not understand is that anybody can pray, teach, and preach, but it is the Holy Spirit that does the drawing. The anointing breaks yokes.

I never will forget when I preached a three-night revival, and on the last night a guy stood up and told me, "if you stop preaching something is going to happen to you." I had no intention of quitting, but after hearing him say that I wasn't going to quit. There are so many things that I could share about God's favor in my life. I have experienced Him doing so much to, for and through me. It has inspired me to walk by faith and not by sight. He saved me, elevated me, healed me and has fought many battles for me. Sometimes I pray that people do not do me wrong because I know God is going to intercede. I have seen Him do it! Once again, this is not me or anything I prayed for, it is the Almighty staying true to His word.

I am grateful to God for every kind of favor and incident where favor has worked on my behalf, big, small and everything in between. I acknowledge it, too. I was sitting at work one morning when a business owner called to inform me that I had won a new flat screen television and could pick it up that day. He had no idea it was my birthday. That was a good way to start celebrating! Of course, my daughter claimed the television. My son carried it from the car, and my daughter pulled it right into her room and connected all the cables that came with it. We were not in the market for a television at that time, but God allowed us to get one at no cost and my children were able to enjoy the benefits of that bit of favor.

I have stated this before and I am sure I will again. There is no way I can neglect to praise the Lord. When I think about how good God is, praise just bursts forth. I tell people to not only praise God for what He can do for you, but get to know Him intimately and praise Him for who He is. This is what I have learned to do because I know He is everything to me.

God thought it was advantageous, even favorable, for me to be born. If I had not been born, I would not be able to share my story with you. If I had not been born, I would not be able to testify that God is a healer. If I had not been born, I would not be here to tell you how He delivered me and longs to do the same for you. Favor has purpose, too. I know it was God's favor that chose me to beat cancer. I hear people say all the time that favor is not fair. Some will probably argue those words because God can and will bless whomever He pleases and He does. By the same token, in my opinion, you deserve to have God's favor if you have used your time in service for the Lord and have obeyed His words. Favor is fair when you have labored with the Lord day in and day out. There is nothing wrong with reaping what you have sown. It is a spiritual principle. If you have God's favor and you know it, just seize the moment.

I HAD A REASON TO PRESS

I always dreamed of getting married and having children. Happily, I did get married in a beautiful ceremony on June 5, 1999, and my husband and I talked about having children shortly after.

Beginning a family would prove to be considerably more difficult than the courtship, engagement and marriage. After my yearly checkup at the Women's Clinic, the doctor informed me that I had abnormal cells that needed attention. Without it, there could be adverse results or eventually turn into cancer. He also told me that I had four fibroid tumors and my chance of getting pregnant would be slim.

That really frightened me and was excruciatingly disappointing. Subsequently, I made the appointment to have the laser surgery to freeze the abnormal cells. After the surgery, the doctor reiterated that it still may be difficult for me to have children. Even after the previous warning, his reminder almost sent me into panic mode. Oddly, I was able to keep it together. I went on with life, but I prayed.

A couple of years later, I took a home pregnancy test. To our delight, it was positive. Finally, I was pregnant! My husband and I were so excited. We told our families, and they were excited, too. The next day I called to make an appointment with my doctor so I could confirm my pregnancy. My appointment was set a month away. Two weeks before the appointment, I started to have pain in my side. I called the doctor to let him know what was going on. Of course, he said that was normal and I had nothing to worry about.

On the day of my appointment, I started to feel a little sick and very uneasy. I went to the bathroom, and I noticed spotting, which made me increasingly worried, but I waited until my husband picked me up from work, and we went to my doctor's appointment which was 45 minutes away. We arrived and were taken back somewhat quickly. The nurse proceeded with the ultrasound. Noticing the expression on her face, I could tell something was wrong. She left the room for about 15 minutes then she returned with my doctor and she said, "I'm sorry Bobbie. It is going to be a loss." I felt something break in me and a well of tears and emotion spilled. My husband tried to console me, but it was a vain effort. He was able to keep his composure in front of others, but when we got to the car, he broke down as well. We both cried. We mourned together.

My husband called each of our families. I was grateful he did because, at the moment, I didn't want to talk to or see anybody. I just wanted to be still and to try to see past the fog that seemed to be covering everything. However, there wasn't much time for that. The doctor had scheduled a Dilation and Curettage (D&C) procedure for the next day, but I was still processing what had happened. When we got home, I locked myself in our bedroom. I could hear our families gathering in the house, but I did not want to come out of the room. My husband had to literally pull me into the living room where everybody was. Once I reached everyone, I broke down again. I kept replaying the news the nurse gave me in my head. Each time I did brought on a new wave of sadness.

Later that night, I started to have severe cramps. I told my husband I needed to go to the emergency room because something was definitely not right. Before I left home, I had a painful urgency to go to the bathroom. When I did, clots of blood came spilling out and I almost passed out. My husband nervously, but quickly, ushered me out of the house and into the car. After we were both inside, he started to drive as fast as the car could go. I was in extreme pain, but my husband's fast driving had most of my attention. It felt like we were traveling at the speed of light. Both my mind and body were leaning and swerving. I almost stood up in the car. My husband called the hospital to alert them that we were coming. So, when we got there the staff immediately got me prepped for D&C procedure. Everything was moving way too fast.

The miscarriage and the surgery left a painful memory. One I would have to live with forever. I lost my first child, an experience I do not wish on anyone. However, three months later the Lord gave me beauty for ashes. He blessed me to get pregnant again. This time I had a really good pregnancy and people could see my excitement. On my delivery day, I was somewhat carefree, at least until I started to have contractions four minutes apart. I remember it just like yesterday. I drove myself to my mom's house because she told me that she had cooked pinto beans and Jiffy cornbread. Unknown to my mom and sister, I was still having contractions, but I sat down at the table to eat anyway. When they noticed, my mom yelled, "Girl you better get up from that table!" I did, and my sister drove me to the emergency room. This time I delivered a precious baby boy. Everybody fell in love with him. We named him after his dad. Since he was a junior, I nicknamed him RJ. My mom was his baby sitter for an entire year before I put him in daycare. I really didn't want to enroll him then, but I knew it was time. Since RJ was a really active child, I wanted to give my mother a break. Just like a first-time mother, I cried the first morning I dropped him off at the daycare center.

During this time, I was pastoring Brassell Chapel A.M.E. Zion Church which was about forty-five minutes from our house. My husband worked at the fire department. His schedule was considered odd to most, but was normal for a fire fighter. He worked twenty-four hours on, and then he would be off forty-eight hours, which meant it was just me and RJ, traveling to and from the church and all around most of the time. Even more so, we lived in the country, and I hated to stay at the house when he had to work all night. I heard every cricket, every breeze and every leaf that fell from each tree.

Three years later, the Lord blessed me to get pregnant again. I used to hear other mothers say that they were sick the whole nine months. In my mind, I would be thinking, "This can't be true. They have to be giving out false information." I soon began to believe every word that they said. I was sick the entire nine months with my daughter. I threw up every single day, even the morning that I was scheduled for an emergency Caesarean section. At one point, I started to think that God was punishing me for something. I made a vow to never have any more kids. That is how sick I was. I had to have an emergency C-Section because my daughter was breached on my delivery date, and she hadn't dropped any. My doctor didn't want to risk me going into labor while the baby was breached. After my doctor read the risk of the C-Section, I almost changed my mind. My husband and I decided that I could get a tubal ligation. I think my doctor thought that I made the decision to get a tubal on my own. He asked me really loudly while locking his eyes with my husband, "Bobbie didn't you say that you wanted a tubal?" I said, "Yes, I did."

As things were settled, our baby girl made her arrival into the world. Our son was three years old at the time and was head over heels about his little sister. We were all excited about the new addition to the family and the newest chapter we were beginning.

When my daughter turned four months old, I started to have trouble breathing. I went to the doctor, and he told me that I had a lung infection. He wrote me a prescription for antibiotics and one for pain medicine. It became harder and harder for me to breathe, and then I started to have night sweats. I didn't know what was going on. I went back to the doctor several more times to get chest x-rays, and I kept getting the same answers. I started to get frustrated because I knew something was wrong with me and the doctors kept giving me false diagnoses. I began to think that I was crazy, but I knew I wasn't. I went walking one day just to ease my mind. I almost passed out on the track and I drove myself to ambulatory care. They sent me to the nearest hospital by ambulance because my heart was in distress. Again, the doctor didn't find anything wrong. Finally, one day I was at work and I started hurting really bad, and I was short of breath. I told my supervisor that I was hurting, and I needed to go to the hospital. I left work and went to the Mediquick Care Center. I told the doctor to refer me to the hospital so I can go get another chest x-ray. The doctor said you just have fluid around your lungs. I told the doctor that I was about to die. She knew I was serious so she did write the referral for me to go to the hospital. They did another chest x-ray, but the results didn't come in until two days later. When the doctor called, I was at the hospital with my baby sister who was battling cancer at the time. The doctor told me that the x-ray did show a mass in the middle of my chest, and she could not read the report, so she was setting me up to see a specialist later that afternoon.

I went to the specialist that evening. My husband was at work, but he asked me if I wanted him to come to the specialist's office. Thinking it was not anything serious, I said, "No." However, my husband decided to come to my appointment anyway, and I was so glad that he did. The specialist told me that I had a form of cancer called lymphoma, which is a blood cancer. I could not believe that. I almost passed out. My husband and the doctor were both trying so hard to comfort me, but I was inconsolable. My sister was already in the hospital battling cancer, and here I am with cancer, too. My baby was six months old, and my son was three. The doctor told me that I had that tumor in my chest when I was pregnant with my daughter.

More upset, I realized, the doctor told me that he was going to send me to the best he knew. He did just that, and I had a major biopsy. The tumor was in the middle of my sternum. Because the tumor was so big and close to my heart, the surgeon had to go through my ribs. That was the most painful procedure that I ever had to endure. I was supposed to be in the hospital for three days, but I had to stay over a week because of my slow recovery time. I still could barely breathe. The doctor thought it was because of the large tube they put down my throat when I was in surgery. I told my husband that it was something else going on. My doctor sent a specialist in to check my vocals out just in case. My husband had gone to the cafeteria to get something to eat. The specialist came in and told me that he had to put a tube in my nose and run it all the way down to my throat. I thought I wasn't going to be able to because I was scared. I whispered me a quick prayer. God gave me the strength to endure it. I was so glad that I did. The specialist told me that I had scar tissues blocking over half of my windpipe. I had to have surgery immediately once again. When my husband was coming back in the room, they were rolling me out the room. He didn't know what was going on. I could see the panic on his face when the doctor gave him an explanation.

My doctor told me how quickly I could go home was dependent on me and my resilience. I wasn't ready to go home at all because I was still in so much pain and I was afraid that something may happen. All kinds of thoughts were going through my head. Fortunately, the biopsy reported that the cancer was localized in one spot in my chest. I was relieved. When the doctor called and told me that, it gave me confidence and I was encouraged to fight. I completed six months of chemotherapy administered every twenty-one days. I had radiation every day during the seventh month. I was so sick. I was hospitalized four times while I was taking the chemotherapy. At one point, I wanted to give up. I had already lost sixty pounds. My baby had to get shots, and the doctor told me I couldn't be around her for a week because she was a threat to me. My sister kept my baby the whole week. She brought her to see me one day. However, I could only look at her through the glass window. That was painful. It was a different kind of pain, one I had never felt before. It took the Lord using my three-year-old son to give me some sense of hope. I will never forget what he said. My son had witnessed me in pain and throwing up every day. One day he came and laid his hand on me and said, "Lord, heal my mommy, and let her live." That gave me the strength that I needed to really fight. The Lord showed me right then and there that I had a reason to press, a reason bigger than myself to keep on keeping on. I had two babies and a husband that were counting on me. Let me encourage you, if you are reading this, know that someone is counting on you, too. Don't give up and don't give in. Your breakthrough is coming.

REFLECTIONS AND MEMORIES

Memories! Many are really good, but then there are those we would much rather forget. Whether good, bad, happy or sad, they are all part of what makes us who we are.

Once when it snowed, my sister, brother and I all decided to go play deep in the woods. We were passing by a branch, and the branch bounced back and hit me in my left eye. It scared me really bad and I was unable to see anything out of my eye. My sister ran home in the knee-deep snow to tell our parents what had happened while my brother guided me out of the woods. The further we walked, the more I started to gain a little eyesight in my eye. It was extremely watery and blurry, but I saw my dad running towards us in the snow. I could see the fear in his eyes. He said my sister just burst through the kitchen door screaming. He had no inkling what he would find when he reached us, but he was determined to get to us and do whatever he had to do. I had a big cut under my eye, but I thank God that I didn't lose my eye. Gratefully, it is all just a memory now.

When I was five years old, we lived in an older, four-room, wood-frame home right off a curve on the main highway. I was ashamed of our house. All my friends had nice brick houses. I would never invite any of them to our house because it was in such bad condition. On top of that, we lived so close to the road I would have nightmares every night, dreaming that a car or truck was crashing right into our house and killing all my family. I would repeatedly tell my mom how afraid I was to live in that house. She had the same response each time, "Stop thinking like that." Well, one night I was almost asleep, but was interrupted by screeching tires. It was obvious a car was trying to stop. I just knew the car was going to crash into our house, but

God spared us that night. Although the car missed our house, it crashed into our neighbors' living room. I ran outside after all the commotion to make sure my neighbors were safe. They said they were in their bed and the front of the car stopped just before it hit the bed where they slept.

After we moved out of the house that was right off the highway, we moved into a five-room house right in the middle of a farm. The house belonged to my dad's boss. There were fields all around the house and pastures that had cows in them. I told my dad that summer that I wanted to work to make my own money. He said, "OK." His quick response almost made me tell him never mind. I knew I had put my foot in my mouth, but I did not retract my request. So, when school was out for summer, my dad told me he had jobs for me, my sister, and my mom. We left with him in his work truck the next morning when he left for work. He drove us to the cotton field, gave each of us a hoe and told us what row we were assigned. There were other workers out there as well. We had to hoe and chop cotton until three or four every evening. I was about to pass out absolutely. I went to the truck about twenty times each day to get water. On the fourth day, I got too hot. I went to sit on the back of the truck. My dad wasn't there at the time, but I saw his work truck pulling in off the road. I didn't have time to run back to my row before he saw me. When he did, he yelled at me in front of all those field workers. He told me to stop being lazy and get back to work. I wasn't lazy. I was hot. I told him I would stay home and fix lunch for them. I could not do that anymore.

In the fall we had to pick big bags of pecans. That was good money, but I didn't like that either. I made my mind up after experiencing that kind of work to finish high school, go to college and get a job that was easier on the body, but paid well.

During my last year of high school, I became close to my counselor. I shared situations with her that were going on at home and she shared many things to help me cope. Sadly, my dad died before my senior year. He didn't get a chance to see me or my sister graduate. I told my counselor that I wanted to leave the state to go to college. I needed to change environments so I could clear my head of all the things I had experienced. My plans were to go to Princeton College in New Jersey because I have an aunt that lived in Hackensack, New Jersey. She had been planning for me to come there since the beginning of my senior year in high school. About two weeks before I was supposed to leave, we decided that I should attend a college in Mississippi. That may have been best, but I only had two weeks to try to get into a school. My counselor worked tirelessly to get me in a college before registration concluded. I finally got accepted to Alcorn State University in Lorman, Mississippi. I'm indebted to Mrs. Shirley Brown, my counselor, for that and more. Again, God's hands were in my plans. Know that if you trust Him, He will open doors for you, even at the last minute.

Depression tried to find me when I couldn't find a job in my field after graduating from college. I completed many applications. No one called me in response to any of them. I wondered if all those years in school had been in vain. I finally decided to take any job that became available to me. I had already completed two internships with the federal government, but I had not heard from my applications submitted to them either. Once I began working at the University of Mississippi for five dollars an hour, the United States Department of Agriculture called and offered me a job in St. Louis. I had never been out on my own, and I didn't have any money to move there, so I declined the job. I later regretted doing that, but all things were still working for my good. I worked at the University for two years, and then I began working with the Federal government again, this time for the Department of the Interior, U.S. Fish & Wildlife Service. I started working for them in 1998 and I am still employed with the agency today. Thank God for consistency and stability. Proudly, I have been working with the agency for twenty-two years. I received my twentieth-year service plaque and pin a couple years ago. One of my friends told me that they have changed jobs over seven times, and, surprisingly, I am still at the same job.

I feel fortunate to have this job. It has allowed me to travel all over the country. I've had the opportunity to travel to Washington, D.C., Tampa, Miami, Clear Water,

Florida, the Everglades, New Mexico, Las Vegas, Arizona, Colorado, West Virginia, Atlanta, Alabama, Louisiana, Arkansas, Texas and other areas. The latest travel was to my dream destination, Hawaii. I completed a detail there. I fell in love with the blue water. The people were so friendly, and I made lasting friendships while I was there.

Another milestone while working with U.S. Fish & Wildlife was that I was asked to travel to Nashville, Tennessee to model our uniforms for our catalog. They told me to ask another co-worker to come with me. We had our own personal stylist and makeup artist. I felt like a celebrity. It really made my day when the stylist told me she had to go buy clothes for an actual celebrity when she finished our photo shoot. That was something that I will never forget. My blessings were overtaking me. God was giving me more than I had asked, thought or imagined.

WHY AM I HERE

I am blessed to not look like what I have been through, but I am a product of all my experiences. Believe me, there was a point in my life when I did look like what I was going through and more. Thank God it was not meant to last forever, and I am here. In either state, I was here on purpose for a purpose. I'm here because it was destined January 29, 1974 that I would be here now to write this book as a source of release for myself and as encouragement and inspiration to others. I'm here because someone needs to read some of what I've had to endure so they can examine my life and see I have not simply been dealt a bad hand, but the hand of God has guided me through it all.

I'm here because I would play a role in the deliverance of my family, the one I was born into biologically. In the process, I would learn to love God, pray to Him fervently and trust Him to reign in every situation we faced.

I'm here because the Lord allowed my husband to find me. Together, we have made our own family, lived our own unique story and are creating our own legacy.

I'm here because every reader needs to know the outcome of everything that I had to endure in my life, especially the emotional childhood. My family is now doing great. My mom is a changed lady. My older sister Lisa is married and has two kids. My baby sister may not be here in the physical, but she left a beautiful daughter, and we all have contributed to her upbringing. Her name is Calandria Crawford. She will be attending college this fall.

I'm here because I can talk to those who have lost fathers, brothers, sisters and mentors from personal experience with compassion and understanding. I'm also here to attest to the fact that God will do a great work and turn things around in the lives of mothers who have fallen prey to the pressures of life.

I'm here because God would use me to pray for many of the ones who once belittled me. I'm here to be an example of the love of God working through people without conditions.

I'm here because God knew that my god sister Claudette Avery and god son CJ Avery would need me in their life. He knew that my friends Vanessa Person and Sharon Bland would need my prayers.

I'm here because God knew that I would be the one to see my friend, Syreeta Kee, struggling to hold onto the back tire of her black SUV after it flipped, crashed through a concrete bridge, fell into a deep creek and became submerged in the contaminated water on a dreary

Sunday morning. Several people had stopped and were looking over the bridge, thinking the worst. But, I'm the one who saw her and ran, tumbling and sliding, to her as far as I could. It was cold and raining and the only way to get to her was to swim out into the water. The only problem was that I could not swim. Still, I was about to jump in the water, but I'm glad that she used all the breath she had left to tell me not to do that. Even though He sent a host of angels afterwards, God wanted me there. He wanted me there to pray and remind her that she was worth dying for and she was worth saving. This is true for all of you.

I'm here because the Spirit of the Lord is upon me; He has anointed and appointed me to preach His Good News to the poor; He has sent me to heal the brokenhearted and to announce that captives shall be released and the blind shall see, that the downtrodden shall be freed from their oppressors, and that God is ready to give blessings to all who come to him. *(paraphrased from Luke 4:18 TLB)*

Everyone reading this needs to know that there is a reason you purchased this book, not to mention a reason why you are here. Like me, you were destined to be. Surrender to God's will for your life. God has a purpose and a plan for you. Jeremiah 29:11 tells us all, "For I know the plans I have for you," declares the LORD, "plans to prosper you and not to harm you, plans to give you hope and a future.

The devil tried to take me out so many times, but God intercepted his play. If I had the chance to rewind life and do it all again, I would not take anything that I've been through back because it has caused me to see that I serve a true and living God. He knew that I would have a story to tell. That is why I'm "Destined to be Here."

www.ingramcontent.com/pod-product-compliance
Lightning Source LLC
Chambersburg PA
CBHW020037040426
42331CB00031B/865